AMERICA GOES TO WAR

THE CIVIL WAR

TIMELINES, FACTS, AND BATTLES

By Craig Boutland

Published in 2023 by The Rosen Publishing Group, Inc.
2544 Clinton Street, Buffalo, NY 14224

Editor: Lindsey Lowe
Children's Publisher: Anne O'Daly
Design Manager: Keith Davis
Picture Manager: Sophie Mortimer

Picture Credits:
Front Cover: Everett Collection/Shutterstock.com
Key: t = top, b = bottom, c = center
Alamy: Album 26, Atomic 19, Everett Collection 61t, Niday Picture Library 26, 61b; Bridgeman Images: Christie's Images 36, Peter Newark 56; Franz-Marc Frei: 32; Library of Congress: 10t, 11b, 13, 15, 16-17b, 21b, 23, 24, 25, 28-29c, 28-29b, 29b, 30, 31, 33t, 33b, 34t, 35t, 35b, 38t, 38b, 41b, 42, 43, 44, 46t, 47t, 51, 58t, 59, 60t, 60b, Adam Cuerden 22-23, 46-47; Public Domain: British Library 41cr, Mike Cline 41cl, Heritage Auctions/restored by Adam Cuerden 10b, Metropolitan Museum of Art 40t, New York Public Library 48, Philadelphia Museum of Art 41t, Photographic History of the Civl War 28t, Rama 16-17t, Scientific American 17t; Robert Hunt Library: 50, 53; Shutterstock: Everett Collection 11t, 37, 45, 49; Topfoto: The Granger Collection 27; U.S. Government: National Portrait Gallery 34b, U.S. Navy 28c, 29t; U.S. National Archives: 5, 6, 7, 8, 9, 12, 14, 18, 22t, 39, 40b, 52, 55.

Cataloging-in-Publication Data

Names Boutland, Craig.
Title: The Civil War: timelines, facts, and battles / Craig Boutland.
Description: New York : Rosen Publishing, 2023. | Series: America goes to war| Includes bibliographic references, index and glossary.
Identifiers: ISBN 9781499473858 (pbk) | ISBN 9781499473865 (library bound) | ISBN 9781499473872 (ebook)
Subjects: LCSH: United States—History—Civil War, 1861-1865— Juvenile literature
Classification: LCC E468 B68 2023 | DDC 973.7/3—dc23

Manufactured in the United States of America

CPSIA Compliance information: Batch #CWRYA23. For further information contact Rosen Publishing at 1-800-237-9932.

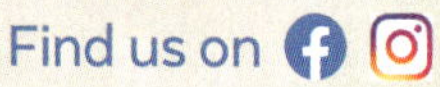

CONTENTS

Introduction

One of the bloodiest conflicts in U.S. history, the Civil War pitted American against American in what became known as the "war between brothers."

With the nation divided by contrasting attitudes towards slavery, Southern states began to secede in late 1860 in an attempt to preserve their lifestyle and economy. Led by President Abraham Lincoln, the North went to war to preserve the Union. It was only with the Emancipation Proclamation of September 1862 that the abolition of slavery became an expressed war aim of the North.

The Course of the War

The South went on the offensive early, coming close to invading the North. The Union slowly gained the advantage, however, as it exploited its industrial strength and railroads in order to arm and transport its troops, and as it gained control of rivers that led like highways to the heart of the Confederacy. The South's "high-water mark" came at the Battle of Gettysburg in July 1863, the largest battle of the conflict and its turning point. After the close-run Union victory, the South never threatened to invade the North again. Northern forces entered the South, bringing devastation and great suffering to civilians. By the time Southern general Robert E. Lee surrendered to future president Ulysses S. Grant after nearly five years of fighting, more than 600,000 Americans were dead.

About This Book

This book focuses on the five years of the conflict, from 1861 to 1865. It contains two different types of timelines. Along the bottom of the pages is a timeline that covers the whole period. It lists key events and developments, color coded. Each chapter also has its own timeline, running vertically down the sides of the pages. This timeline provides more specific details about the particular subject of the chapter. IN FOCUS spreads give more details of important people, weapons, and events.

Soldiers in the war were often very young, like this Confederate private. In many cases, sons fought alongside their fathers.

Causes of the Conflict

To both the North and the South, the Civil War was justified as self-defense: defense of the Union for the North and defense of Southern freedoms for the South.

➔ The premises of a dealer of enslaved people in Virginia in 1860. Slavery had existed in all 13 of America's colonies.

TIMELINE **1861 JANUARY–MARCH**

KEY: Politics | Land War | Sea War

January

January 2 South Carolina Confederate troops occupy Fort Johnson in Charleston Harbor.

January 9 Mississippi Mississippi becomes the second state to join the Confederacy.

January 10 Florida Florida leaves the Union.

January 11 Alabama Alabama is the fourth state to leave the Union.

January 19 Georgia Georgia leaves the Union.

January 26 Louisiana Louisiana is the sixth state to leave the Union.

At the heart of the quarrel was Black slavery. Slavery had existed in the Americas since the earliest days of the 17th century, when the labor of enslaved people was a key feature of the Southern plantation system. Colonists grew crops such as tobacco, sugar, rice, and cotton that required many workers, which the trade of enslaved people provided cheaply.

At independence, there were about 600,000 enslaved persons in the new country. Almost all of them were in the South. In many northern states, slavery became illegal. In the South, meanwhile, cotton plantations came to dominate the economy—and they relied on slavery.

Expansion of the Country

The rapid growth of the United States in the first half of the 19th century brought the question of slavery to the fore. As new territories joined the Union, would they be slave or free states?

In 1819,

KEY DATES

1787 Northwest Ordinance outlaws slavery northwest of the Ohio River.

1803 The Louisiana Purchase of French-owned land doubles the size of the nation.

1820 Missouri Compromise: Missouri enters the Union as a slave state.

1846-1848 Mexican War adds territory in the West and Southwest.

1854 Kansas-Nebraska Act creates two new territories, with the settlers entitled to decide on the issue of slavery.

1860 Election of Abraham Lincoln as president brings slavery issue to a head.

← When they arrived in the United States, enslaved people were kept in cramped cells while they waited to be sold.

February

February 4 Alabama Southern leaders write a new constitution for the Confederate States of America. Jefferson Davis is chosen as president.

February 7 Alabama/ Mississippi The Choctaw Indian Nation makes an alliance with the Southern states; other native peoples follow in 1861.

February 26 Alabama The Confederate Congress establishes a general staff for the Army of the Confederate States.

March

March 4 Washington, D.C. Abraham Lincoln is inaugurated as 16th president of the United States; he announces "I have no purpose, directly or indirectly, to interfere with the institution of slavery in the States where it exists."

March 11 Alabama The Confederate Congress adopts the Constitution of the Confederate States of America.

Dred Scott

In 1846, the Missouri enslaved man Dred Scott sued for his freedom on the grounds that he had lived for many years in a free state. The Supreme Court finally decreed in 1857 that Scott was still an enslaved person, Black people were not U.S. citizens, and that laws banning slavery in parts of the U.S. were illegal. The ruling appalled many in the North.

Missouri applied to join the Union as a slave state. Many northerners objected, but Missouri's wish was granted. As a balance, Maine became a free state. In the so-called Missouri Compromise, slavery was forbidden north of latitude 36° 30'.

The Abolition Movement

The slavery debate grew more bitter. In the North, abolitionists were a small but powerful minority against slavery. Southerners believed they threatened the whole basis of southern life. In 1852, Harriet Beecher Stowe's novel *Uncle Tom's Cabin* intensified the debate with its powerful exposure of the cruel conditions of slavery.

The Kansas-Nebraska Act of 1854 allowed people in those territories to decide for themselves

➔ An enslaved woman is sold at auction. Families were often sold separately and split up forever.

TIMELINE 1861 APRIL–JUNE

KEY: Politics | Land War | Sea War

April

April 12 South Carolina The Confederate troops attack Fort Sumter in Charleston Harbor.

April 13 South Carolina Fort Sumter surrenders to the Confederates. The Civil War has begun.

April 15 Washington, D.C. President Lincoln calls for the Northern states to raise an army of 75,000 troops to fight the South.

April 19 Washington, D.C. President Lincoln orders a naval blockade of the Southern states.

April 23 Virginia Major General Robert E. Lee becomes commander of land and naval forces in Virginia.

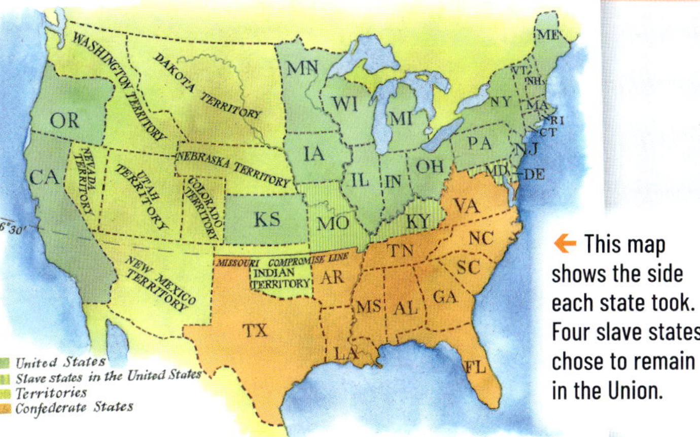

This map shows the side each state took. Four slave states chose to remain in the Union.

John Brown

John Brown saw slavery as a sin against God. In October 1859, he led a raid on the federal arsenal at Harpers Ferry in Virginia, hoping to start a uprising of enslaved people. He was caught and hanged for murder. His bearing at his trial gained him sympathy in the North. More Southerners concluded that it was time to leave the Union.

whether to be free or slave states. Abolitionists and slavers came to blows over the future of "Bleeding Kansas." Meanwhile, the Dred Scott case (see opposite page) and John Brown's failed attempt to start an uprising of enslaved people in 1859 encouraged abolitionists in the North.

John Brown was a passionate idealist motivated by his deeply held religious beliefs.

A New President

The election of Abraham Lincoln as president in November 1860 dismayed the South. Lincoln and the Republicans, who drew their support from the North and the West, had campaigned strongly against any extension of slavery. To accept Lincoln as president was, to most Southerners, acceptance of second-class status in the Union. Secession, leaving the Union, seemed the only answer.

May 9 Britain
Great Britain announces its intention to remain neutral during the war.

June 10 Virginia
West Virginia breaks from Virginia and the Confederacy, and joins the Union as a separate state.

May — **June**

May 20 North Carolina
North Carolina becomes the last state to leave the Union.

June 10 Virginia
In one of the first battles of the war, 1,200 Confederates defeat 3,500 Union troops at Big Bethel.

Abraham Lincoln

The 16th president of the United States kept the Union together through the Civil War.

The election of Abraham Lincoln was the direct trigger for the Southern states to secede and form the Confederacy. Lincoln was a lawyer in the state of Illinois. His powerful speaking had made him a national figure during the seven debates he had with Stephen Douglas in 1858, when the two men were running for the Senate. When Lincoln was elected president in 1860, he claimed that he would take any steps necessary to keep the Union together, but his election was clear evidence to the Southerners that slave-owning states were in a minority within the nation.

1

Lincoln's Moral Authority

Abraham Lincoln proved himself to be a successful war leader partly because he had strong principles and great moral authority. His Emancipation Proclamation of January 1863 declared that all slaves in the Confederate states should be free. It started the process that ended slavery in the United States. In the Gettysburg Address, a short speech made by Lincoln at Gettysburg in November 1863, he laid out clearly and powerfully the intended aims for which the North was fighting.

President Lincoln was assassinated as the Confederate armies were surrendering. His death left a vacuum at the heart of government that was not properly filled, which subsequently led to many of the problems of the postwar period.

2

3

4

THE RAIL CANDIDATE.

KEY DATES

February 12, 1809 Abraham Lincoln is born in a log cabin in Kentucky.

1834 Lincoln wins election to the Illinois House of Representatives. He will serve four terms.

1858 Lincoln makes his famous speech, including the biblical quotation "a house divided against itself cannot stand" during the Lincoln-Douglas electoral campaign of 1858.

April 15, 1861 Newly inaugurated president, Lincoln calls for 75,000 volunteers to recapture bases and forts taken by the Confederacy.

November 8, 1864 Lincoln is reelected president in a landslide victory, winning all but three states.

April 14, 1865 John Wilkes Booth shoots the president while Lincoln is watching a play at Ford's Theater. Lincoln dies the next day.

1 Stephen Douglas in 1859. The Lincoln-Douglas debates in 1858 brought LIncoln to national prominence.

2 A colored illustration of John Wilkes Booth shooting Lincoln at Ford Theater in 1865. The assassination shocked the nation.

3 Lincoln as president. Although he had little military experience, he was a successful war leader.

4 A cartoon of 1860 pokes fun at the Republican Party candidate, showing him as a homespun politician who had spent much of his life splitting rails.

Secession and First Shots

Between December 1860 and June 1861, 11 Southern states seceded from, or left, the Union. They believed they had the right to leave if the federal government abused its power.

In this engraving, Confederates bombard Fort Sumter from the shores of Charleston Harbor on April 13, 1861.

TIMELINE **1861 JULY–SEPTEMBER**

KEY:  **Politics** **Land War** **Sea War**

July

July 2 Wisconsin Union forces push back Confederates in the Battle of Hoke's Run.

July 21 Virginia The First Battle of Manassas, also called the First Bull Run, is the first major battle of the Civil War. The Confederates resist a determined Union attack, and Union troops retreat in panic toward Washington, D.C.

August

August 10 Missouri The Battle of Wilson's Creek is the first battle west of the Mississippi River; the Confederates win an encounter that leaves 2,500 casualties.

August 26 West Virginia Confederates force Union troops to retreat at Kessler's Cross Lanes.

A Northern cartoon attacks the seceding states for pulling apart the Union, which is shown as a cow.

KEY DATES

November 6, 1860 Abraham Lincoln is elected president.

December 17, 1860 South Carolina votes to leave the Union.

January 1861 Alabama, Florida, Georgia, Louisiana, and Mississippi leave the Union.

February 1861 Texas secedes. The Confederate States of America is created.

March 4, 1861 Lincoln is sworn in as president.

April 12, 1861 The first shots of the Civil War are fired as Confederate troops attack Union-controlled Fort Sumter.

April 17, 1861 Virginia secedes from the Union.

May 20, 1861 North Carolina becomes the last state to leave the Union.

The emergence of the Republican Party in the North in the late-1850s pushed moderate Southerners to consider secession. Republicans would keep slavery out of new territories in the West, which secessionists believed would lead to the abolition of slavery. As the 1860 election drew near, they argued that the election of the Republican candidate, Abraham Lincoln, would justify secession.

The Upper South Holds Back

Only the seven states of the Deep South had viewed Lincoln's election as sufficient cause

September

August 28–29 North Carolina Union troops capture shore batteries around Hatteras Inlet in an amphibious raid.

September 12–15 West Virginia In the Battle of Cheat Mountain Summit, Robert E. Lee, future hero of the Confederacy, is defeated despite having stronger forces than the enemy.

September 13 Missouri Confederates begin a week-long battle that forces the surrender of Union troops in Lexington.

September 17 Missouri The Confederate campaign in Missouri continues with another victory, in the Battle of Liberty.

September 19 Kentucky A large Confederate force raids the Union guerrilla training base in Barbourville, but finds the camp largely empty.

Pierre G.T. Beauregard

General Pierre Gustave Toussaint Beauregard became a popular Confederate hero for his role at Fort Sumter. Born into a Creole family in Louisiana, he graduated from West Point. After Louisiana left the Union in 1861, Beauregard resigned from the U.S. Army. After Fort Sumter, he took command of the Confederate army in northern Virginia. He saw action in every major theater of the war, making general after the First Battle of Bull Run.

for secession. The slave states of the upper South generally shared the proslavery views of the seceding Deep South states, but they knew that if war came, much of the fighting would take place on their soil. Slavery was not as important to the economies of Maryland, Delaware, Kentucky, and Missouri as it was to the Deep South cotton-producing states.

Lincoln's Response

Lincoln's inaugural address (opening speech) repeated his intention not to interfere with slavery where it already existed. But he issued a warning to the seceded states, promising that the federal government would "hold, occupy, and possess" forts and other properties that were still under Union control in the South. This soon focused attention on Fort Sumter, a federal fort on an island in Charleston Harbor, South Carolina.

→ An engineer, P. G. T. Beauregard was one of eight full generals to join the Confederate army.

Confederate Dilemma

Confederate president Jefferson Davis realized that the Union could not keep a garrison

TIMELINE 1861 OCTOBER–DECEMBER

KEY: Politics | Land War | Sea War

October

October 21 Missouri Battle of Fredericktown. Union troops push back Confederates to win control of southeastern Missouri.

October 21 Kentucky Some 7,000 Union troops defeat Confederates in the Battle of Camp Wildcat.

October 21 Virginia In the Battle of Ball's Bluff, Union forces fail to cross the Potomac River at Harrison's Island to attack Leesburg.

November

November 7 Missouri Ulysses S. Grant, future commander of all Union armies, defeats Confederate forces at Belmont near the Mississippi River, but withdraws after a counterattack.

November 8 Kentucky In the Battle of Ivy Mountain, a large Union force fights off an ambush and pushes the enemy back into Virginia.

on Confederate soil without compromising the independence of the Confederacy. If he did not act, others in the South might. He ordered General Pierre G. T. Beauregard to take the fort before the Union could send in reinforcements. On April 12, 1861, Confederate guns opened fire. Two days later the fort surrendered.

An engraving showing a crowded secession meeting in Charleston, South Carolina. South Carolina was the first state to leave the Union.

More Secession

The next day, Lincoln called up 75,000 state militia, so signaling his intention to fight. This set in motion a second wave of secession, including Virginia. Virginia was crucial to the South. It was the most populous Southern state, it was located in a critical position across the Potomac River from Washington, D.C., and it had the greatest industrial capacity of any Southern state. Meanwhile, four slave states—Delaware, Kentucky, Maryland, and Missouri—never left the Union.

November 8 Cuba A diplomatic incident begins when Union sailors illegally seize Confederate officials from a British ship; the Union apologizes after British protests.

November 19 Oklahoma Confederate troops attack and defeat Unionist Creek and Seminole Indians at the Battle of Round Mountain.

December

December 9 Oklahoma Confederates continue to harass retreating Creek and Seminole at the Battle of Chusto-Talasah.

December 21 At the Battle of Dranesville, Union troops defeat "Jeb" Stuart's Confederate cavalry in northern Virginia.

Rifles and Pistols

The weapons of the Civil War marked a period of transition in small arms design.

The Civil War took place at a turning point in military technology. Most soldiers were still trained to fight in lines in the open, as in the Napoleonic wars of 1805–1815, but the weapons they were armed with had improved dramatically. The basic weapon used by infantry soldiers still only fired a single shot, but it was accurate to a range of about 300 yards (274 m), rather than the 100 yards (91.5 m) of the Napoleonic wars, because there were grooves, or rifling, inside the barrel. These made the bullet spin, which made it more accurate over open distances. Soldiers soon realized they needed to find cover when on the attack. Cavalry and infantry attacks over open ground suffered huge casualties. The most famous of these disastrous attacks was Pickett's Charge at the Battle of Gettysburg in 1863.

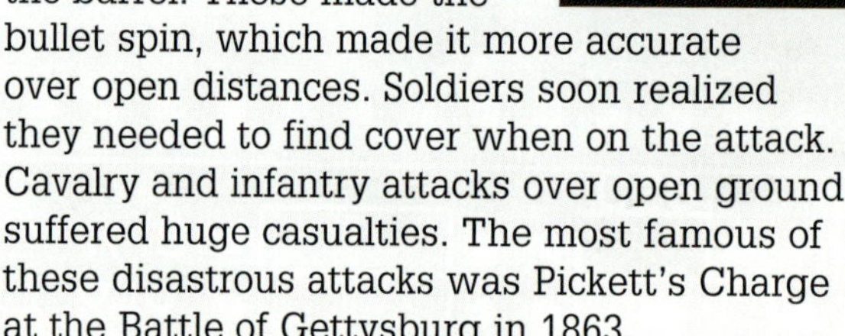

Repeating Weapons

Although most infantry were armed with a single-shot weapon, Samuel Colt had invented the revolver in the 1830s. This was a pistol that could fire six shots before needing to be reloaded, but it was not accurate over long range. However, technological improvements were made during the Civil War and some Union units began using repeating rifles that could fire several bullets before being reloaded. The most famous of these was the Spencer repeating rifle, which had a magazine containing seven bullets and was used from 1863 onward. It replaced the Sharps carbine, which could only fire one shot before reloading.

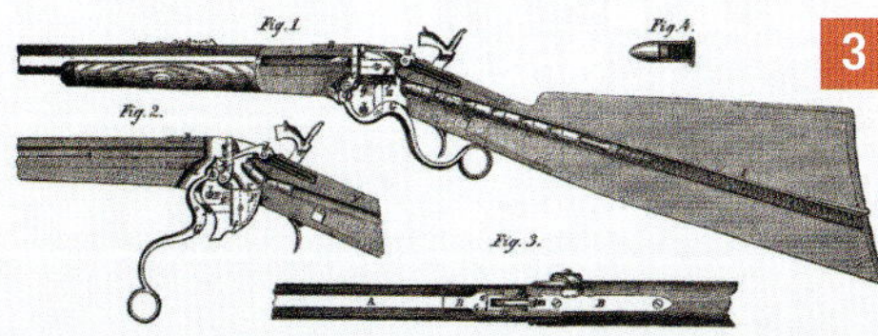

3

KEY DATES

February, 1836 Samuel Colt takes out a U.S. patent on his new six-shot revolver.

1861 The Civil War armies go into the conflict using a mixture of smoothbore and rifled muskets. The standard Union weapon becomes the Springfield Model 1861 muzzle-loader. More than 1 million were produced, costing $15 each.

1863 Most Union cavalry regiments begin using the Sharps single-shot carbine.

July, 1863 The Spencer repeating rifle with a magazine of seven shots is demonstrated to President Lincoln, who orders the Union Army to buy it. The army initially fails to do so, believing that the weapon will use up too many valuable bullets.

1864 Gatling guns are used by the Union Army at the siege of Petersburg. Union officers had to buy their own, because the army was unwilling to fund the new weapons.

1 An 1860 Colt revolver, a weapon that had changed pistol design by allowing a user to fire more than one shot before reloading.

2 A Union cavalryman fires his single-shot Sharps carbine while his companion reloads at the Battle of Middleburg.

3 A contemporary diagram showing how the Spencer repeating rifle had a magazine inserted in the butt. This held seven bullets that could all be fired before the rifle needed reloading.

The First Battle of Bull Run

Also called the First Battle of Manassas, the First Battle of Bull Run was one of many large-scale encounters between the Union and Confederate armies.

Similarities in the uniforms and flags of the two sides added to the confusion of the battle.

TIMELINE **1862 JANUARY–MARCH**

KEY: Politics | Land War | Sea War

January

January 3 Virginia Union gunboats bombard Confederate coastal batteries guarding the Potomac at Cockpit Point.

January 5–6 Maryland Confederate general "Stonewall" Jackson fails to force the surrender of the town of Hancock.

January 10 Kentucky At the Battle of Middle Creek, Union troops halt the Confederates' 1861 offensive in Kentucky.

January 18 Arizona The Confederate Territory of Arizona is created from part of New Mexico.

January 19 Kentucky Union counterattacks push the Confederates back from Logan's Crossroads to Murfreesboro, Tennessee.

A photograph of Bull Run Creek showing an army pontoon bridge and Union troops.

In July 1861, both sides were sure that the war would be short and relatively bloodless, and that one grand campaign would decide the war in their favor. The first Battle of Bull Run showed that the war would be long and bloody.

Battle Preparations

By early summer, Lincoln faced huge popular pressure to send his large army of volunteers to march on the new Confederate capital at Richmond, Virginia. General Irvin McDowell protested that his army of citizen-soldiers was not ready, but public demand was irresistible, and he was ordered to set out for Richmond in early July.

KEY DATES

July 16 McDowell's Union troops head toward Manassas.

July 18 The Confederates use Manassas Gap Railroad to reinforce Beauregard's troops.

July 18 Union troops try to cross Bull Run Creek.

July 21, morning Union troops cross Bull Run Creek.

July 21, late morning Confederates pushed back to Henry Hill.

July 21, afternoon Fighting continues on Henry Hill. Two Confederate armies unite just as the Confederates appear to be losing. Jackson attacks.

July 21, late afternoon Exhausted Union troops begin to retreat.

July 21, evening Union retreat descends into chaos as Confederates shell road to Washington.

February

March

February 6 Tennessee Union general Ulysses S. Grant captures Confederate Fort Henry. The Union now controls the Tennessee River as far south as Alabama.

February 16 Tennessee Union troops under Grant capture Fort Donelson and take around 15,000 Southern prisoners.

February 25 Tennessee Nashville becomes the first Confederate capital to fall to Union troops.

March 8 Virginia The Battle of Hampton Roads. The Confederate ironclad CSS *Virginia* sinks two wooden Union ships and badly damages another.

March 9 Virginia CSS *Virginia* returns to Hampton Roads but is met by the Union ironclad USS *Monitor*. A four-hour, close-range battle ends in stalemate.

March 17 Virginia Union troops ship to the tip of the Virginia "peninsula," marking the start of the Peninsular Campaign.

Battle Details

1. On July 18, a Union detachment tried to cross Bull Run Creek. It was pushed back in a skirmish that lasted all afternoon.

2. On July 21, the main Union force made a flanking movement, crossing Bull Run Creek at Sudley Ford at 9:30 a.m. After fighting on Matthew's Hill, the Confederates fell back to Henry Hill by late morning.

3. Fighting continued on Henry Hill. After reinforcements arrived, Thomas "Stonewall" Jackson led the Confederate counter-attack. By the late afternoon, Union troops were in retreat.

McDowell's target was the equally inexperienced Confederate army, commanded by Pierre G. T. Beauregard, McDowell's classmate at West Point. His army was stationed just north of Manassas Junction close to Washington, on Bull Run Creek. Manassas was a key Confederate supply depot and railroad stop, and would be a valuable conquest for Union armies.

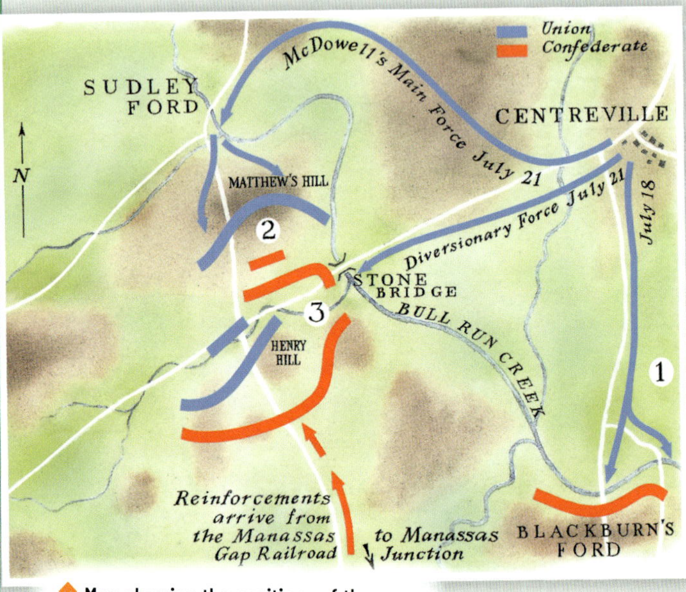

Map showing the positions of the two armies at the First Bull Run.

TIMELINE 1862 APRIL–JUNE

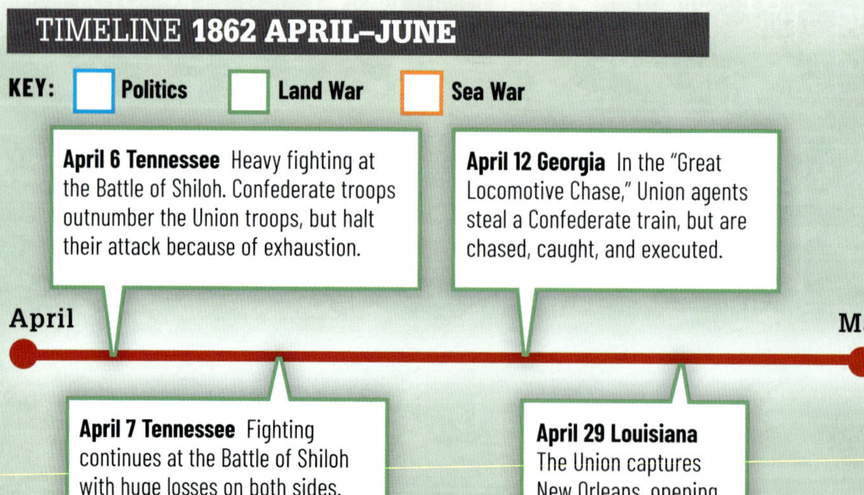

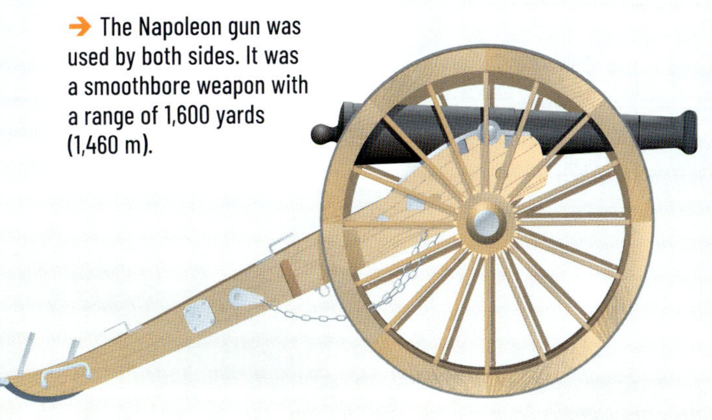

The Napoleon gun was used by both sides. It was a smoothbore weapon with a range of 1,600 yards (1,460 m).

"Stonewall" Jackson

Thomas J. Jackson was a West Point graduate who joined the Confederacy out of loyalty to his home state, Virginia. His nickname came from his stand at Bull Run, which also saw him promoted to major general. His accidental death in 1863, when he was shot by his own men, was a huge blow to the Confederate cause.

Main Battle

McDowell attacked first. His army pushed the Confederates back to Henry Hill. By the afternoon, they were almost defeated, but reinforcements arrived. Commander Thomas J. Jackson led a counterattack that earned his nickname of "Stonewall." By evening, the Union army was beaten.

First Bull Run was smaller than later battles (1,900 Confederate and 2,800 Union casualties), but it was the initial exposure to combat for many of the war's commanders. It had proved the importance of railroads in troop movements and also dispelled all illusions of a quick resolution to the war.

Thomas "Stonewall" Jackson became a hero because of his battle tactics.

May 15 Virginia Five Union gunboats advance up the James River toward Richmond, but are forced back by Confederate gunfire.

May 25 Virginia A Confederate victory at Winchester relieves pressure on Richmond.

May 31 Virginia The Battle of the Seven Pines is drawn, with heavy losses on both sides.

June

June 6 Tennessee Union ships launch an attack on Memphis and capture the city after a short battle.

June 12 Virginia "Jeb" Stuart leads 1,200 Confederate cavalry on a three-day ride to seize 165 Union men on the Virginia Peninsula outside Richmond, Virginia.

June 25 Virginia At Oak Grove near Richmond, Confederates launch a counterattack that is the first of the Seven Days' Battles.

Robert E. Lee

This son of Virginia proved himself a master of the battlefield in many Civil War encounters.

Robert E. Lee had been a successful commander in the Mexican-American War (1846–1848). In 1861, he reluctantly decided to throw in his lot with the State of Virginia although he believed secession was wrong. After a period as a military adviser to the Confederate president, Jefferson Davis, Lee was given command of the Army of Northern Virginia in 1862 and proved himself an excellent battlefield commander. Part of his strength was that he knew how to make full use of the talents of his subordinates, such as Thomas "Stonewall" Jackson, James Longstreet, and cavalry commander J. E. B. Stuart. Lee was popular with his soldiers, who called him "Master Robert."

Victories Against the Odds

Although he was usually outnumbered, Lee fought off Union attacks toward Richmond at the Seven Days Battle, at Fredericksburg, and at Chancellorsville. He was, however, unsuccessful in two attempts to take the war into the North, suffering defeat at Antietam in 1862 and Gettysburg in 1863. Lee took responsibility for the defeat at Gettysburg, apologizing for his decision to order "Pickett's Charge."

In 1864, Lee won tactical victories at the battles of the Wilderness and Spotsylvania during the so-called Overland Campaign, but Union superiority forced him to give ground. His army was finally pinned down at Petersburg. His forces ebbed away and Lee finally surrendered in April 1865.

KEY DATES

January 19, 1807 Robert Edward Lee is born in Westmoreland County, Virginia.

March 13, 1847 Lee is wounded at the Battle of Chapultepec during the Mexican War.

1861 Lee resigns from the U.S. Army and joins the Confederacy. However, he writes: "I can anticipate no greater calamity for the country than a dissolution of the Union."

May, 1863 Although vastly outnumbered, Lee wins the Battle of Chancellorsville, his greatest victory. His key subordinate, Thomas "Stonewall" Jackson, is killed in the battle.

April 19, 1865 Lee surrenders Confederate forces at Appomattox Courthouse.

October 12, 1870 Lee dies in Lexington, Virginia.

1 Thomas Jonathan Jackson, the most brilliant of Lee's subordinate commanders, was a master of battle tactics.

2 The painting created in 1887 by Thure de Thulstrup shows the disastrous Pickett's Charge at the Battle of Gettysburg.

3 Robert E. Lee during the Civil War. A revered commander during the war, he became an advocate for reconciliation between North and South after the war.

River War

The South had thousands of miles of rivers, and control of them was to be the key to Union victory. The Union navy fought for supremacy over these vital river links.

Riverboats moored at White House Landing, a key Union supply base during the 1862 Peninsular Campaign.

TIMELINE **1862 JULY–SEPTEMBER**

KEY: Politics | Land War | Sea War

July

July 1 Washington, D.C.
The Union government introduces income tax to help pay for the war.

July 11 Washington, D.C.
General Henry Halleck replaces General George B. McClellan as commander of the Union army.

July 13 Washington, D.C.
Lincoln drafts the Emancipation Proclamation, freeing the enslaved people in the South.

July 17 Washington, D.C.
The Union government opens the way for the formation of Black units in the Union army.

August

August 14 Virginia
The Army of the Potomac begins to withdraw from Harrison's Landing, ending the Peninsular Campaign.

The Union navy had a growing fleet of wooden sailing ships and steamships, plus new ironclad gunboats. It could thus overwhelm Confederate river defenses, preventing the South from using its rivers for transportation. Once the rivers were secured, the Union could use them to move troops and supplies through Tennessee, Mississippi, and Louisiana. The Confederate navy, suffering from shortages of men and materials, could not match its Union opponents.

River War in the West

The river war in the West occurred roughly in three phases. During the first, from January to March 1862, Union forces concentrated on the Tennessee and the Cumberland Rivers. The campaign included one of the war's bloodiest encounters at Shiloh Church, near Pittsburg Landing on the Tennessee. In a two-day battle,

KEY DATES

February 6, 1862 Union gunboats capture Fort Henry after a bombardment.

February 16, 1862 Union troops capture Fort Donelson with help from gunboats. The Tennessee and Cumberland Rivers are now in Union hands as far as Corinth, Mississippi, and Florence, Alabama.

March 9, 1862 The drawn naval battle between ironclads CSS *Virginia* and USS *Monitor* at Hampton Roads leads to acceleration in ironclad shipbuilding program.

April 16–28, 1862 Union naval victory takes Fort Jackson and St. Philip on the Mississippi.

July 4, 1863 The last Confederate fort on the Mississippi surrenders; Union naval forces now control the whole river.

1864 Red River Expedition ends in failure for Union troops trying to move up Red River and find a way into Texas.

← The Union river gunboat USS *Fort Hindman* patrolled the Mississippi River.

August 29 Virginia The Second Battle of Manassas (Second Bull Run) lasts two days and ends in a Confederate victory that defeats a Union attempt to capture Richmond.

September

September 17 Maryland The Battle of Antietam ends in a draw after Confederates resist a Union attack at the Bloody Lane for four hours. Both sides suffer enormous casualties.

September 18 Missouri Ten Confederate prisoners are executed in what is known as the Massacre at Palmyra.

September 22 Washington, D.C. Lincoln issues the Emancipation Proclamation. It will take effect on January 1, 1863.

September 24 Tennessee In revenge for Confederate shelling of his gunboats, Union general William Sherman orders the destruction of every house in the town of Randolph.

Battle of Shiloh

The battle fought on April 6–7, 1862, began when Confederate general Albert S. Johnston's army surprised a Union army at Shiloh Church, Tennessee. Some of the fiercest fighting of the war took place in a peach orchard. The buzzing noise of bullets gave it the name "the Hornet's Nest." The battle cost the South 10,700 killed and wounded for no gain, while the North narrowly avoided defeat at a cost of 13,000 casualties.

nearly 24,000 soldiers were killed or wounded for little gain on either side.

The second phase of the river war, between March 1862 and July 1863, saw the Union try to gain control of the Mississippi River.

The least successful of the three phases of the river war came from March to May 1864 on the Red River, when Union troops were almost stranded at Alexandria, Louisiana, when water levels fell.

River War in the East

In the east, the York and the James Rivers were crucial in the 1862 Peninsular Campaign. In March 1862, Union general George B. McClellan moved his army via Chesapeake Bay to Fortress Monroe, Virginia. He used river transports to establish

→ River transportation was invaluable for moving Union troops to war theaters in the South.

TIMELINE 1862 OCTOBER–DECEMBER

KEY: Politics | Land War | Sea War

October

October 3–4 Mississippi
Union forces in the city of Corinth resist an attack by 22,000 Confederates.

October 4 Texas
After a Union blockade, the port of Galveston is forced to surrender to Union forces.

October 8 Kentucky
Union victory in the Battle of Perryville forces the Confederates to retreat from Kentucky into eastern Tennessee.

November

November 7 Washington, D.C.
Abraham Lincoln appoints Ambrose E. Burnside as commander of the Army of the Potomac to replace George B. McClellan, whom Lincoln thinks is not aggressive enough.

An engraving of the Battle of Shiloh depicts Union troops fighting to recapture artillery.

a supply depot at White House Landing, only 20 miles (32 km) from Richmond.

Battle Details

1. Johnston's Confederates make a surprise attack early on April 6. Johnston is killed; Beauregard takes command.

2. Confederates push Union troops back to the river.

3. Grant's Union army is reinforced during the night.

4. Union troops counterattack on April 7 and make progress. In late afternoon, Beauregard orders a withdrawal.

Natural Defenses

Rivers were a major obstacle for Union armies in Virginia. Most rivers run west to east through the state, while Union troops generally advanced north to south, apart from the Peninsular Campaign. Rivers formed a natural line of defense for the Confederate army.

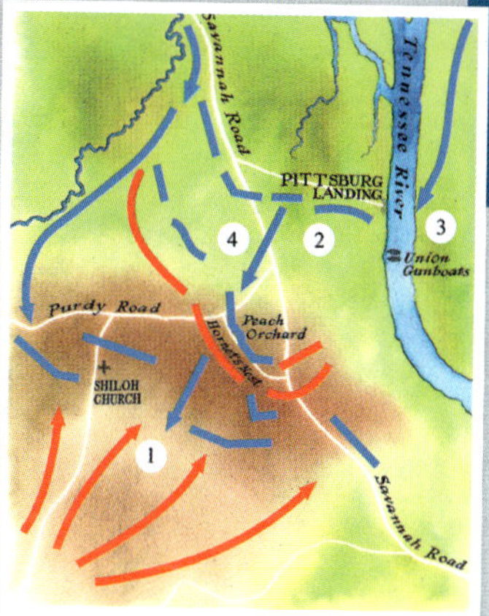

This map shows the main stages (see above) of the Battle of Shiloh.

December 13 Virginia
Eager to prove himself, Burnside tries to cross the Rappahannock River and advance on Richmond. In the Battle of Fredericksburg, he loses 6,500 men in 14 failed attacks on Confederate lines.

December 31 Tennessee
Union troops eventually prevail at the Battle of Murfreesboro after being initially forced to fall back.

December

December 7 Tennessee
The Battle of Hartsville. A Confederate attack defeats Union troops guarding the Cumberland River, opening the way to western Tennessee and Kentucky.

December 14 Virginia
The Battle of Fredericksburg. Burnside is persuaded by his officers not to launch more attacks. It is a great Confederate victory.

Merrimack and *Monitor*

The first encounter between ironclad vessels took place at Hampton Roads in March 1862.

A major part of the Union plan to defeat the Confederacy was to isolate the seceded states by a naval blockade. As the Union had kept control of the vast majority of naval vessels, this was a promising and ultimately successful strategy. However, the Confederacy had taken control of the most modern vessel in the U.S. Navy. This was the steam-driven frigate *Merrimack*, in the Gosport navy yard near Norfolk, Virginia. Renamed the CSS *Virginia*, this vessel was converted into a warship protected by iron plates, firing explosive shells and with a ram attached.

Head-to-Head

On 8 March 1862, CSS *Virginia* took on the wooden Union vessels blockading the Hampton Roads and sank two of them. The Union Navy had, however, constructed its own ironclad vessel, the USS *Monitor*. This mounted another technological innovation, a revolving turret. The following day, *Monitor* fought an inconclusive duel with *Virginia* in the first battle between ironclads. The Confederate army abandoned Norfolk in May, and *Virginia* was destroyed to stop it falling into Union hands. *Monitor* ended its days in December 1862, sinking with the loss of 16 men while it was being towed to assist in the blockade of North Carolina.

KEY DATES

1855 The *Merrimack*, a steam-powered frigate, is launched by the U.S. Navy. It does not have any protective iron plating.

1859 *Gloire*, a French ironclad warship, is launched. Its armour protects it from most cannon balls. It was propelled by steam power and so not reliant on the direction of the wind.

August 3, 1861 The Union navy begins work on its ironclad *Monitor* when it learns that the Confederates are working on the hull of *Merrimack*. John Ericsson is the key designer. *Monitor* is completed in 101 days.

August 5, 1864 Four Union navy ironclads take part in the Battle of Mobile Bay.

1865 The Union navy has over 50 ironclad monitors, based on the design of the original USS *Monitor*.

1 The crew of USS *Monitor* pose for a photograph in front of the revolving turret that gave it an ability to fire in all directions.

2 A Union vessel burns after being attacked by CSS *Virginia* during the first day of the naval battle at Hampton Roads.

3 Sailors abandon ship from the sail-powered vessel USS *Cumberland* as it is attacked by the ironclad CSS *Virginia*.

4 A painting of the epic duel between the two ironclads. They were unable to inflict fatal damage on each other.

5 USS *Monitor* was low in the water and eventually sank because heavy waves proved too much for the ship to cope with.

6 John Ericsson, the Swedish-born designer of the ironclad USS *Monitor*.

Home Front

For Southern civilians, the effects of the war were more immediate than for Northerners. Their lives changed totally while life in the North was largely unaffected.

A Northern engraving shows Southern women urging their men to go to war, then suffering the consequences later.

TIMELINE 1863 JANUARY–MARCH

KEY: Politics | Land War | Sea War

January

January 1 Washington, D.C. The Emancipation Proclamation comes into effect. The Civil War becomes a struggle to free the slaves as well as to preserve the Union.

January 20–22 Virginia
The Union army of the Potomac advances toward Lee, but rain softens the ground and the "Mud March" is bogged down.

January 29 Idaho
Union soldiers seeking revenge on Native American allies of the Confederates kill over 380 Shoshoni at the Boa Ogoi camp.

January 30–31 South Carolina
Two Confederate ironclads break the Union blockade of Charleston.

February

Most Southerners welcomed the war, and men enlisted enthusiastically. With three out of four eligible men serving in the Confederate army, the Southern home front was largely a world of women, children, and enslaved people. Women often had to take charge of family farms when the men were away fighting. On some plantations, owners' wives took over day-to-day affairs. Many found managing the enslaved people the most challenging aspect of their new duties.

Twenty Slave Law

Early in the war, a new law exempted white men from military service if they ran plantations with more than 20 enslaved persons. Poorer families who had no enslaved people or whose women were forced to labor in the fields when their husbands were away resented this favoring of the upper classes.

Shortages and Refugees

By 1862, food shortages in the South were severe. This was partly the effect of the Union

KEY DATES

1860 On the eve of war, the North is home to 21.6 million white individuals, 248,000 free Black individuals, and 430,000 enslaved individuals; the South has 5.4 million white individuals, 133,000 free Black individuals, and 3.5 million enslaved individuals.

1862 Confederate draft is introduced. Southerners suffer from severe food shortages, while the Union economy continues to prosper.

1863, March The Union draft is introduced.

1863, July Antidraft riots in Northern cities.

1864 Ulysses S. Grant's plan to "squeeze the South" creates 250,000 refugees.

Students at the Academy of Fine Arts in Philadelphia making a flag. Such activities helped to keep up civilian morale.

February 3 Tennessee Having failed in a mission to disrupt shipping on the Cumberland River, Confederate cavalry make an unsuccessful and bloody attack on the Union garrison at Dover.

March

March 3 Washington, D.C. The Union government introduces the National Conscription Act, which is deeply unpopular with those forced into military service.

March 6 Virginia The unpopular Confederate Impressment Law gives officers the right to take food from farmers at fixed prices.

March 8 Maryland Confederate guerrilla leader John Mosby leads a raid behind enemy lines to Fairfax Court House, taking Union prisoners and horses before returning to Confederate lines.

Bread Riots

By spring 1863, stores of grain in the South were running out. Prices rose rapidly. People accused stores and the government of hoarding supplies. In some places, "bread riots" broke out. The worst was in Richmond, Virginia. Several hundred women smashed store windows and seized food and goods. Confederate president Jefferson Davis came to calm the rioters. Despite his appeals, they refused to leave until he threatened to order the militia to open fire, when they dispersed.

blockade and partly the result of a poor distribution system that prioritized military supplies. There were shortages of salt—for preserving meat—iron for railroad tracks, coffee, and manufactured cloth. Prices rose sevenfold, so many people could no longer afford even basic foods.

In addition, as many as 250,000 Southerners became refugees as Union armies invaded the South. Rural families whose homes and farms lay in the path of the invading troops fled to cities such as Richmond, Columbia, and Atlanta, which became overcrowded and chaotic as a result.

The North

By comparison, the Union home front fared well. The North had a far larger industrial base, and people on the home front had a key role in keeping the economy buoyant. Many men enlisted, but enough remained to manage farms or work

→ This is an example of the classical Greek Revival style of plantation homes built before the war.

TIMELINE 1863 APRIL–JUNE

KEY: Politics | Land War | Sea War

April

April 2 Virginia
"Bread riots" break out in the Confederacy because of high food prices.

April 17 Mississippi
Union cavalry raid Mississippi, tearing up railroad lines before heading south to Baton Rouge, Louisiana.

May

May 2 Virginia
During the Confederate victory at the Battle of Chancellorsville, "Stonewall" Jackson is killed by one of his own men.

May 3 Virginia
The Battle of Chancellorsville. A renewed Confederate attack pushes back Union forces.

An enslaved family in Hampton, Virginia, in 1861. Their daily life was strictly regulated.

in industries. They were joined by a growing number of women, mainly as unskilled laborers. Women also entered other work from which they had been barred. It was almost unheard of for women to work as government clerks or nurses, for example, but during the war it was commonplace.

Civilian Fundraising

Many Northern cities held fairs to raise funds to provide medical supplies for wounded soldiers and other types of relief. The first such fair was held in Chicago on October 27, 1863. It ran for two weeks and drew 5,000 visitors. President Lincoln donated the draft of the Emancipation Proclamation, which was the fair's main attraction. It sold at auction for $3,000.

This house was a hospital after the Battle of White Oak Swamp in June 1862.

May 4 Virginia
Union reinforcements cannot prevent a great Confederate victory at Chancellorsville.

May 14 Mississippi
Union troops capture Jackson, the state capital, and destroy its factories and railroads.

May 18 Mississippi
Ulysses S. Grant's Union troops begin the siege of Vicksburg.

June

June 9 Virginia
After a battle of massed cavalry charges, Confederates eventually gain victory at the Battle of Brandy Station.

June 14 Virginia
Victory in the Battle of Winchester allows Lee's Army of Northern Virginia to invade the North with 75,000 men.

June 16
Lee's army crosses the Potomac River, intending to win a decisive victory in Pennsylvania and capture Washington, D.C. Southern morale is high.

Wartime Elections

Even during the most intense fighting, the Union States managed to hold elections.

When war broke out, both the Republicans (who dominated the free states) and the Northern Democrats supported the attempt to defeat the Confederacy. However, by 1862 there was a faction of the Democratic Party that was opposed to continuing the war. These Democrats made gains in the elections of 1862, winning an additional 28 seats in Congress and taking the governorship of New York.

1

The National Union

The most extreme of the Democrats who opposed the war were known as "Copperheads." Two congressmen from Ohio, Clement L. Vallandigham and Alexander Long, were the most prominent of the Copperheads. They called for an immediate end to the fighting.

By 1864, Union armies were winning victories and opposition to the war declined. In November 1864, the Union states held elections in which President Lincoln ran for a coalition of Republicans and "War Democrats." His running mate was Democrat Andrew Johnson. This coalition was known as the National Union Party. It easily defeated the Peace Democrat candidate, former serving general George B. McClellan.

2

3

4

KEY DATES

May 31, 1864 Radical Republicans call a convention in Cleveland, Ohio, where they nominate John C. Fremont for president. They claim Lincoln is incompetent.

June, 1864 The main Republican Party becomes a coalition incorporating so-called "War Democrats." Democrat Andrew Johnson is chosen as Lincoln's running mate.

June 9, 1864 Lincoln is nominated for president by the Republican Convention. On the first vote some delegates voted for Ulysses S. Grant but the final nomination was unanimous.

July 22, 1864 The Battle of Atlanta confirms the success of Union armies against the Confederacy and bolsters Lincoln's position.

August, 1864 The Democratic Party chooses George McClellan as its candidate for president, with George C. Pendleton as the nominee for Vice president.

November 8, 1864 Lincoln wins 55 percent of the popular vote, and wins the Electoral College 212–21.

1 Abraham Lincoln's second inauguration, after his sweep of most of the Northern states in the election of 1864.

2 General George B. McClellan ran as candidate for the Peace Democrats in 1864, even though he supported the war.

3 A hostile cartoon portrays the Lincoln cabinet as a corrupt organization, functioning through the printing of money.

4 A National Union poster distributed before the election of 1864, showing Abraham Lincoln and his running mate Andrew Johnson.

Emancipation Proclamation

Lincoln's Emancipation Proclamation came into effect on January 1, 1863. It declared "all persons held as slaves within a State" were "thenceforward, and forever free."

African Americans wait up for New Year's Day 1863, when the new law comes into effect.

TIMELINE **1863 JULY–SEPTEMBER**

KEY: Politics Land War  Sea War

July

July 1 Pennsylvania The Battle of Gettysburg ranges 75,000 Confederates against 90,000 Union soldiers of the Army of the Potomac.

July 2 Pennsylvania During a day of fierce fighting at Gettysburg, Union troops halt Confederate attacks.

July 3 Pennsylvania At Gettysburg, an attack by 15,000 Confederates—Pickett's Charge—fails, marking the effective end of the battle. Some 6,000 men are dead. The Confederate failure is the turning point of the war.

July 4 Mississippi Vicksburg surrenders, thereby splitting the Confederacy in two.

July 13 New York Antidraft riots break out across the North, including in New York City.

Lincoln's decree ensured that the Civil War became a war of Black liberation as well as a struggle to save the Union. Lincoln had often said that his responsibility as president was to suppress the South's rebellion, not to free its slaves. But slavery lay at the very heart of the conflict and had to be addressed. By late 1862, Lincoln judged there was enough public support to incorporate enslaved person emancipation into his policy.

Southern Reaction

The South reacted furiously to the decree that enslaved people under Southern control were free. President Jefferson Davis called it an

KEY DATES

1861 Union army turns away free Black volunteers.

September 17, 1862 Union victory at Antietam gives Lincoln a position of strength to tackle the slavery controversy.

September 22, 1862 The Emancipation Proclamation gives rebellious states an ultimatum to rejoin the Union or all existing slaves will be declared free.

January 1, 1863 The final Emancipation Proclamation is issued.

Spring 1863 Free Black people and former slaves join the Union army.

March 3, 1865 The Freedmen's Bureau is set up.

December 18, 1865 Thirteenth Amendment to the Constitution finally abolishes slavery.

← This painting shows Abraham Lincoln reading the Emancipation Proclamation to the cabinet in July 1862.

August

September

August 20 Kansas Confederate guerrillas led by William Quantrill attack the antislavery town of Lawrence, killing 150 male civilians.

September 6–8 South Carolina A Union marine and infantry assault at Charleston Harbor wins Fort Wagner but not Fort Sumter.

September 19 Tennessee In the Battle of Chickamauga, 65,000 Confederates face 62,000 Union soldiers.

September 20 Tennessee The Battle of Chickamauga ends with Confederate victory; Union forces retreat to Chattanooga, but with 18,000 casualties, the Confederates cannot push home their advantage.

Fort Pillow

Confederate soldiers did not treat African American soldiers fighting for the Union with the respect that they treated white troops. One notorious event was the massacre of Fort Pillow. When Union troops, mostly African Americans, surrendered, the Confederates murdered unarmed men, shouting, "No quarter! No quarter!" Of the white troops, 68 percent were taken prisoner, but only 20 percent of the African American soldiers were imprisoned. A subordinate of Confederate commander Nathan Bedford Forrest said Forrest ordered the prisoners to be "shot down like dogs."

An enslaved person reads news of the proclamation.

"effort to excite servile war within the Confederacy." Davis warned that many Black soldiers serving in Union armies would be tried under the Confederate slave laws.

Northern Reaction

In the North, however, abolitionists, African Americans, and others welcomed the emancipation. Leading abolitionist Frederick Douglass congratulated Lincoln on "this amazing approximation toward the sacred truth of human liberty." However, many others pointed out that the proclamation was very limited, freeing enslaved people only in areas that were still under Confederate control and

An illustrated print of Lincoln's Emancipation Proclamation.

TIMELINE **1863 OCTOBER–DECEMBER**

KEY:  **Politics** 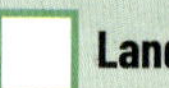 **Land War**  **Sea War**

October

October 5 South Carolina The CSS *David* damages the USS *New Ironsides* in Charleston Harbor with a spar torpedo.

October 14 Virginia An error by Confederate general A. P. Hill leads his men into an ambush at the Battle of Bristoe Station.

October 15 South Carolina The *H. L. Hunley*, an experimental Confederate submarine, sinks during a training exercise, killing seven of its crew of nine.

November

November 19 Pennsylvania At the dedication of a battlefield cemetery, Lincoln delivers the Gettysburg Address: he promises that "government of the people, by the people, for the people, shall not perish from the earth."

not in the loyal border states or in Union-controlled parts of the Confederacy.

Effect of the Proclamation

Despite its limitations, the proclamation began the process of freeing the South's enslaved people. It did not end slavery—that came with the Thirteenth Amendment in December 1865—but it gave the Union cause a moral force and strengthened it both militarily and politically. It also ended any chance of foreign intervention: no European country was prepared to oppose a crusade against slavery. As for African Americans themselves, they still had many more battles to fight before they would become truly free.

Freedmen's Bureau

Established in March 1865, the Freedmen's Bureau was one of the first federal social service agencies. It was intended to help with every aspect of life for refugees (both Black and white), and newly freed slaves in the South. Its major success was in providing education for freed children and adults, for many of whom it was a first chance to go to school. All today's major Black colleges were founded or helped by the bureau. It closed in 1872 after only seven years of operation.

African American children attend school in a freedmen's village in Arlington, Virginia.

November 23 Tennessee The Battle of Chattanooga begins when Union troops manage to push back the Confederate siege.

November 24–25 Tennessee Union forces at Chattanooga storm Cemetery Ridge to secure the city and its vital food supplies.

December

December 9 Tennessee A 17-day siege of Union troops in Knoxville ends when Confederate forces withdraw after Union reinforcements arrive.

December 14–15 Tennessee The Battle of Bean's Station ends in a Confederate victory over 4,000 Union soldiers.

December 29 Tennessee Cavalry fighting at Mossy Creek sees rebel forces pushed back and the Union in control of the area.

The International War

Lincoln's war cabinet had a difficult task in trying to keep foreign powers from intervening in the Civil War.

A key part of the Union strategy to defeat the Confederacy was to cut it off from the outside world. The Southern States had few industrial centers and many of the materials of war—from bullets to rails for repairing railroads—had to be imported. The policy of European industrialized nations such as Britain and France was therefore critical. Southern cotton was important for European economies, which had an interest in keeping up cotton imports. Lincoln's administration under its secretary of state, William H. Seward, managed a successful set of initiatives that kept these European nations from assisting the South.

1

Mill Workers and Commerce Raiders

The Union attempts to keep European powers out of the war were assisted by many in Europe who were opposed to slavery. Workers in cotton mills in Britain, for example, were prepared to undergo hardship and unemployment rather than help the Southern economy.

Lincoln had less success in preventing the building of ships called commerce raiders. British shipyards built several commerce raiders that attacked Union shipping and tried to break the blockade of Southern ports. The most famous of these was the CSS *Alabama*.

2

KEY DATES

May, 1860 William Seward stands against Lincoln for the Republican Party nomination for president. Seward takes more delegates on the first ballot, but is defeated. Bitterly disappointed, Seward considers resigning from public life.

December, 1860 Lincoln offers Seward the post of secretary of state.

November, 1861 The Trent affair. The Union navy stops a British vessel and arrests two Confederate diplomats travelling on it. Seward persuades Lincoln to release the diplomats.

December, 1861 French forces invade Mexico. Emperor Napoleon III of France wants to recognize the Confederacy. Seward threatens war if he does so.

November, 1862 The United Kingdom agrees not to recognize the Confederacy. France follows suit and withdraws its attempt to recognize the Confederacy.

1 Emperor Napoleon III of France. He wanted to help the South, and tried to use the Civil War to intervene in the politics of Mexico.

2 A group of diplomats from Europe are entertained by William Seward near a waterfall in New York State.

3 CSS *Alabama* is tracked down and sunk off Cherbourg, France, by the USS *Kearsage* in July 1864. This painting is by Edouard Manet.

4 Officers on board CSS *Alabama*, a successful commerce raider built in Britain. Britain later paid compensation to the U.S.

5 A print of the USS *San Jacinto* stopping the *Trent* to arrest two Confederate diplomats, an incident that Seward smoothed over.

6 William Seward. He was unhappy about losing the 1864 Republican presidential nomination, but Lincoln persuaded him to become secretary of state, a vital role.

The Battle of Gettysburg

Over three days, the largest battle of the Civil War was fought between Lee's Confederate army and Meade's Union army at Gettysburg, Pennsylvania, in July 1863.

Confederate Louisiana Tigers advance on a Union battery on the second day of Gettysburg, July 2, 1863.

TIMELINE **1864 JANUARY–MARCH**

KEY: **Politics** **Land War** **Sea War**

January

January 17 Tennessee
The Battle of Dandridge is a Confederate victory but does not seriously harm Union forces.

January 26 Alabama
After a two-hour assault, Confederate cavalry fail to capture Athens, despite their superior numbers.

January 27 Tennessee
A Confederate incursion against Union forces near Dandridge is halted at the Battle of Fair Garden.

February

February 14 Mississippi
Major General William T. Sherman begins a week-long raid that destroys a key railroad junction at Meridian.

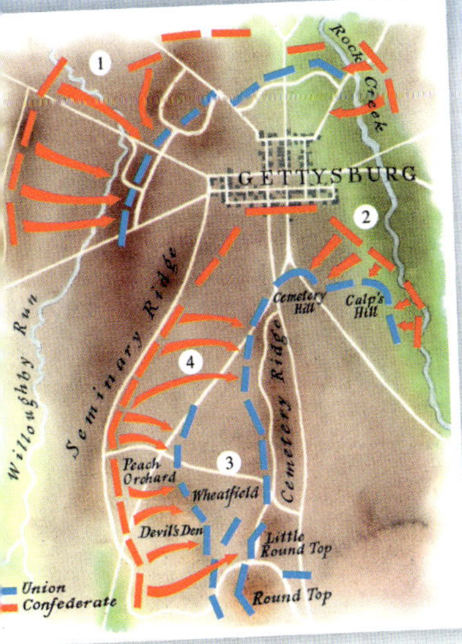

The encounter began almost by chance when foraging Confederate soldiers ran into Union cavalry west of Gettysburg, a town that was always a potential battleground. It was important because it lay at the junction of roads leading to Washington, Baltimore, and Harrisburg, the capital of Pennsylvania. Generals Robert E. Lee and George G. Meade quickly ordered their respective Confederate and Union commanders to concentrate their forces on the town.

BATTLE DETAILS

July 1, 1863 Confederates advance from the north (1) and occupy Gettysburg. Union forces retreat to high ground south of the town.

July 2, 1863 Union forces pushed back as fierce fighting takes place at Devil's Den and Peach Orchard, but Union line holds (2).

July 2, late afternoon Piecemeal Confederate attacks on Cemetery Hill and Culp's Hill make no headway (3).

July 3, 1863 15,000 Confederate troops make doomed frontal assault, later called Pickett's Charge. The failure of the attack marks the end of the battle (4).

July 4, 1863 Lee orders his defeated troops back to Virginia.

Confederate troops advance at Gettysburg on July 3, 1863, in the attack known as Pickett's Charge.

March

February 20 Florida Union forces, including a Black regiment, are forced to give up an expedition to disrupt Confederate supply lines near Jacksonville.

February 22 Georgia The Battle of Dalton is an inconclusive clash at Crow Valley, near Dalton.

March 2 Washington, D.C. Ulysses S. Grant is made commander of all the armies of the Union.

March 14 Louisiana Union troops enter the Confederate Trans-Mississippi Department and capture Fort DeRussy.

March 25 Kentucky Confederates assault the city of Paducah on the Ohio River, but withdraw after heavy casualties.

Photography

The Civil War was the first U.S. conflict to be captured by photography. For the first time, graphic images brought the brutality of war to the home front. Pioneers such as Mathew Brady took images that were printed in many newspapers. Although the images only showed the aftermath of battle—cameras were not quick enough to capture action—they profoundly changed how the public saw the war.

The First Day

Union troops advanced from the south, Confederates from the north and northwest. Union forces were pushed back from Gettysburg and were on the verge of losing the battle when they were rallied by the arrival of reinforcements. By nightfall, the Confederates held the town, but Union forces were secure to the south on Cemetery Hill and Culp's Hill. Both armies reinforced overnight.

The Second Day

By July 2, more than 93,000 Union men were in position on the hills and Cemetery Ridge. Fighting began in the afternoon with a disaster for the Union as III Corps, advancing without orders, was destroyed in savage fighting around the Peach Orchard and Devil's Den. However,

→ A photograph titled "A Harvest of Death, Gettysburg, Pennsylvania" shows dead soldiers awaiting burial after the Battle of Gettysburg.

TIMELINE **1864 APRIL–JUNE**

KEY: Politics | Land War | Sea War

April

April 8 Louisiana A Union advance up the Red River ends when its gunboats are forced to retreat; stranded by falling water levels, the Union force has to build dams to allow the boats to escape.

April 9 Louisiana Union troops retreating from Red River face a Confederate attack at the Battle of Pleasant Hill.

April 12 Tennessee Confederates massacre the Union garrison at Fort Pillow, including 202 of the 262 Black troops. "Remember Fort Pillow" becomes a rallying cry among Black troops.

May

May 3 Virginia Grant moves the Army of the Potomac south to meet Lee's army, but his men have to cross the marshy Wilderness.

May 5 The Battle of the Wilderness. The armies of Lee and Grant fight in thick undergrowth.

Union artillery on the summit of Little Round Top on the final day of Gettysburg.

Union defenses on the high ground held. As night fell, Lee's piecemeal attacks on the Union flanks had made no gains.

The Third Day

On July 3, Lee made a bid to take Cemetery Ridge. At 1:00 p.m., 150 Confederate guns began their biggest artillery bombardment of the war. At about 3:00 p.m., 15,000 troops led by George E. Pickett began Pickett's Charge. Advancing across a mile (1.6 km) of open ground, they were fired on by Union artillery; within 200 yards (180 m) of the front line, the infantry opened up. Only a few hundred Confederates survived. As he rode out to meet the shattered survivors, Lee admitted, "It's all my fault. It is I who have lost this fight." On July 4, he ordered his army back to Virginia. More than 20,000 Confederates were killed, wounded, or missing; Union casualties were 23,000.

The Gettysburg Address

Lincoln's speech in November 1863 at the dedication of a new war cemetery at Gettysburg was one of the most famous in U.S. history. He explained his view of the war as a larger struggle for democracy and equality. He insisted "...we here highly resolve that these dead shall not have died in vain—that this nation, under God, shall have a new birth of freedom—and that government of the people, by the people, for the people, shall not perish from the earth."

May 6 Virginia Brush fires halt the Battle of the Wilderness. Soldiers rescue the wounded; the battle is a draw.

May 11 Virginia The South suffers a huge blow when famed cavalry leader "Jeb" Stuart is wounded and killed at the Battle of Yellow Tavern.

May 12 Virginia One of the bloodiest battles of the war is fought at Spotsylvania Court House; after 24 hours of hand-to-hand combat at the "Bloody Angle," the battle is drawn.

June

June 3 Virginia Only 11 miles (18 km) from Richmond, Union troops begin a major attack on Lee's army at Cold Harbor but suffer 7,000 casualties for no gain at all; Confederate casualties are only 1,500.

June 27 Georgia More Union losses at the Battle of Kennesaw Mountain, where Union forces charge Confederate lines with bayonets.

Ulysses S. Grant

A successful general and the 18th president, Grant also wrote excellent military memoirs.

Ulysses S. Grant distinguished himself as a junior officer in the Mexican-American War (1846–1848) but then resigned from the army. He rejoined in 1861 and took the 21st Illinois Regiment to fight in Missouri. He advanced into Kentucky and then led Union forces that took Fort Henry on the Tennessee River and Fort Donelson on the Columbus River. Grant followed this up by winning another victory at Shiloh in April 1862. President Lincoln defended Grant against his critics saying "I can't spare this man; he fights."

Decisive Victories

Grant and his men took the city of Vicksburg on the Mississippi in July 1863, cutting the Confederacy in two. In November, he led Union forces at the decisive Battle of Chattanooga. After this success Lincoln put Grant in charge of all Union armies. In June 1864, he led a massive force (over 500,000 men) against Robert E. Lee's army. Lee fought a series of battles in which the Confederates lost fewer men, but Grant pressed on remorselessly. He trapped Lee in the railroad center of Petersburg while other Union armies advanced through the Shenandoah Valley and took Nashville. Union soldiers also advanced through Georgia in the winter of 1864. Ulysses S. Grant accepted Robert E. Lee's surrender in April 1865, effectively ending the Civil War.

KEY DATES

April 27, 1822 Ulysses S. Grant is born in Ohio.

September, 1861 Grant is given command of forces in the Mississippi Valley.

April 6-7, 1862 Grant wins the Battle of Shiloh.

July 4, 1863 Grant accepts the surrender of Vicksburg, splitting the Confederacy in two.

March 2, 1864 Grant is given command of all Union armies. He leads Union forces into Virginia and starts the siege of Petersburg in June.

November, 1868 Grant is elected 18th president of the United States.

July 23, 1885 Ulysses S. Grant dies in New York City, having just completed his memoirs, one of the best descriptions of command in warfare.

1 Admiral Porter's fleet of ironclads break through the Confederate blockade of the Mississippi in the siege of Vicksburg.

2 Thure de Thulstrup's painting of the Battle of Shiloh, where Grant suffered early defeats, but regrouped to win a major victory.

3 Grant in 1864, during the period of the Battle of Cold Harbor. Although Lee's Confederate forces still proved tactically superior, Grant refused to admit defeat and eventually managed to push Lee into Petersburg where a long siege began.

March to the Sea

In late 1864, Union general William T. Sherman led his troops on a destructive march through Georgia to the sea and then north through the Carolinas.

A group of Sherman's infantry rest outside some farm buildings they have occupied.

TIMELINE 1864 JULY–SEPTEMBER

KEY: Politics | Land War | Sea War

July

July 11 Washington, D.C.
Concern sweeps the Union capital when Confederate troops reach the city limits.

July 22 Georgia
In Atlanta, the Confederate defenders make an unsuccessful attempt to break the Union siege.

July 30 Virginia
Union troops explode a huge mine beneath Confederate lines at Petersburg, but fail to take advantage.

← Sherman's troops marched 600 miles (960 km) in just five months.

Following his capture of Atlanta, Georgia, on September 3, 1864, Union general William T. Sherman planned to march to Savannah, a port on the Atlantic coast 220 miles (352 km) away. The capture of the port would enable Union ships to supply the army. Sherman also believed the march would damage Confederate morale.

Sherman burned anything of military value in Atlanta—one-third of the city accidentally burned as well—and on November 15, he set out with 60,000 men to march on Savannah.

KEY DATES

September 3, 1864 Sherman captures Atlanta, Georgia.

November 15 Sherman leaves Atlanta with 60,000 men.

December 21 Sherman captures Savannah.

February 1, 1865 Sherman leaves Savannah.

February 17 Sherman captures Columbia, state capital of South Carolina.

March 19–21 Confederates fail to halt Sherman at the Battle of Bentonville.

April 13 Sherman captures Raleigh, state capital of North Carolina.

April 26 Joseph E. Johnston surrenders to Sherman.

← The damage left by the march made Sherman unpopular in the South.

August 5 Alabama
At the Battle of Mobile Bay, a Union fleet takes two hours to defeat the Confederate ironclad *Tennessee* and capture the port; the South still controls the city of Mobile.

September 16 Virginia
Confederate troops steal beef supplies at Coggins Point to feed hungry Southerners.

August — **September**

August 31 Georgia
Sherman moves south of Atlanta to cut the city's supply lines; the Confederates leave the city the next day.

Eyewitness

The behavior of Sherman's soldiers in Columbia, South Carolina, was described by 17-year-old Emma LeConte in her diary: "The drunken devils roamed about setting fire to every house the flames seemed likely to spare.... They would enter houses and in the presence of helpless women and children, pour turpentine on the beds and set them on fire.... The wind blew a fearful gale, wafting the flames from house to house with frightful rapidity. By midnight the whole town was wrapped in one huge blaze."

Unopposed March

The Confederates turned back to Tennessee, leaving few forces to oppose Sherman. He spread his army along a wide path, which made it easier to gather supplies. As the troops advanced, they wrecked railroads and anything else that might aid the Confederate war effort. In many cases, the foraging was accompanied by theft and vandalism. Thousands of lawless stragglers followed the army and were beyond military control. Even Sherman's veterans voiced doubts about the harsh treatment of civilians. Some of the worst-treated civilians were enslaved African Americans who had been liberated by the Union army.

Sherman captured Savannah on December 21, 1864. His next aim was to join forces with Ulysses

→ In this engraving, former enslaved people follow the Union army in late 1864.

TIMELINE **1864 OCTOBER–DECEMBER**

KEY: Politics | Land War | Sea War

October 19 Virginia At the Battle of Cedar Creek, Jubal Early's Confederates rout two Union corps but are defeated when Union reinforcements bolster the line; the defeat breaks the back of the Confederate army in the Shenandoah Valley.

October

October 23 Missouri
In the war's largest battle west of the Mississippi, the South fails to break the Union hold on Missouri.

S. Grant in Virginia and defeat Robert E. Lee's army. Sherman determined to march through the Carolinas. He set out on February 1, 1865.

Sherman in the Carolinas

This march faced more Confederate troops, swampy rivers, and roads turned to mud in the winter rain. Nevertheless, the Union troops surprised the enemy with their rapid advance. The destruction in South Carolina was worse than in Georgia. South Carolina had been the first state to secede and was seen by many Union soldiers as responsible for the war. The state capital, Columbia, was burned on February 17–18, 1865, although who started the fire remains controversial.

In March, Sherman entered North Carolina. The Confederates failed to stop his progress at Bentonville on March 19–21 and a few days later Sherman occupied Raleigh, the state capital. On April 26, General Johnston surrendered. The marches through Georgia and the Carolinas had been decisive. They showed how weak the Confederacy had become, while their destructiveness demoralized the population and hastened its defeat.

These scenes from the "March to the Sea" were published in the North in 1864; Sherman's easy advance was as much of a morale boost for the North as it was demoralizing for the South.

November

December

November 8 Washington, D.C.
Abraham Lincoln is reelected, mainly thanks to the popularity of Sherman's capture of Atlanta in September.

November 25 New York
Confederate agents set fire to buildings in New York City, but fail in their plan to start a general fire.

November 30 Tennessee
At the Battle of Franklin, John Bell Hood's Confederates come close to defeating the Union line, but are ultimately unsuccessful.

December 9 Georgia
Sherman's troops begin to surround the Confederate-held city of Savannah.

December 21 Georgia
Union troops enter Savannah, marking a triumphant end to the "March to the Sea."

Siege Warfare

The capture of Vicksburg was essential if the Union was to regain control of the Mississippi River. From May 1862 to July 1863, Grant's army besieged the city.

A Union battery of mortars lined up at the Siege of Yorktown, Virginia, in April 1862.

TIMELINE **1865 JANUARY–MARCH**

KEY: Politics | Land War | Sea War

January 15 North Carolina Union forces seal off Wilmington, the only major Confederate port still open and the South's last access to the outside world.

January 19 South Carolina Having completed his infamous "March to the Sea," Union general William T. Sherman vows to push through the Carolinas into Virginia and orders troops into South Carolina.

January

February

February 3 Virginia Peace talks are held on board a boat at Hampton Roads, but Lincoln and the Confederate delegates do not reach a diplomatic ending to the war.

Siege warfare was based on tactics developed by European armies over the previous 200 years. It was slow and destructive. First, the enemy position was surrounded. All routes of escape or resupply were cut off, presenting the enemy with a stark choice—surrender or face starvation. The next step was to position siege artillery, of which the most feared was the mortar. Developed specifically for sieges, this short, squat weapon lobbed shells in a high arc to land inside enemy defenses: there was no defence against it.

Vicksburg Under Siege

Union general Ulysses S. Grant targeted Vicksburg from December 1862, but was

KEY DATES

April-May 1862 Siege of Yorktown, Virginia. The outcome is inconclusive.

April-May 1863 Siege of Suffolk, Virginia. The outcome is inconclusive.

May-July 1863 Siege of Vicksburg, Mississippi. Union victory.

May-July 1863 Siege of Port Hudson, Louisiana. Union victory.

August 1864 Siege of Fort Morgan, Mobile Point, Alabama. Union victory.

August 1864 Siege of Fort Gaines, Alabama. Union victory.

April 1865 Siege of Petersburg, Virginia. Union victory.

← The Union army blows a crater in the defenses around Vicksburg in June 1863.

March

February 17 South Carolina As Union troops enter Columbia, bales of cotton are set alight. Fire destroys half the city.

March 2 Virginia Union cavalry capture 1,500 Confederates at Waynesboro, gaining control of the whole Shenandoah valley.

March 3 Washington, D.C. The U.S. Congress establishes the Freedmen's Bureau to deal with problems caused by the sudden freeing of tens of thousands of enslaved people.

March 4 Washington, D.C. President Lincoln makes his second inaugural address, ending with the words, "With malice toward none."

March 13 Virginia Enslaved people are allowed to become soldiers in the Confederacy as the Congress in Richmond passes a law authorizing the use of Black troops.

Siege of Vicksburg

After Grant reached Vicksburg in May 1862, the Union army set up 220 heavy guns to bombard the city day and night. Inside Vicksburg, the civilian population suffered as badly from the shelling as the defending soldiers. Many took refuge in caves dug out of hillsides behind the city. Food ran out by late June. Pemberton was also running out of ammunition. Grant refused any terms except unconditional surrender, which came on July 4, 1863.

foiled by the city's defensive position, guarded by the Mississippi. It was not until May 1863 that he managed to trap the Confederate army of John C. Pemberton inside the city. Grant fought off a relieving army led by Joseph E. Johnston and besieged the city.

Digging Trenches

Grant's army dug 15 miles (24 km) of trenches to protect them against artillery fire from within the city. The besieging infantry dug trenches closer and closer to the enemy's forward defenses in preparation for the opening of a breach through which an assault could be made. The diggers protected themselves behind a sap-roller, a large basket filled with earth.

→ Grant launched a two-pronged attack to take Vicksburg into Union control.

TIMELINE 1865 APRIL–MAY

KEY:  **Politics** **Land War**  **Sea War**

April

April 2 Virginia Confederates retreat from Petersburg and, on April 3, from their capital at Richmond.

April 9 Virginia Surrounded and outnumbered, General Robert E. Lee signs the surrender of his army to General Ulysses S. Grant at Appomattox Court House.

April 14 Washington, D.C. Abraham Lincoln is shot by John Wilkes Booth and fatally wounded while at the theater with his wife.

April 15 Washington, D.C. Lincoln dies from his wounds.

April 26 North Carolina Joseph E. Johnston surrenders Southern forces in the West.

April 27 Tennessee The Union riverboat *Sultana* sinks on the Mississippi River; 1,400 soldiers on their way home from battle drown.

Using Explosives

Breaches were also made by digging a tunnel, filling it with gunpowder, and blowing it up. The Union army used this method twice, at Vicksburg in June 1863 and 13 months later in July 1864 at the Siege of Petersburg, Virginia. On both occasions, however, Union troops who advanced across the crater caused by the explosion could not get out and became sitting targets. Southern engineers meanwhile dug tunnels beneath the Union tunnels, which could then be collapsed or blown up.

Lack of Supplies

For all the bloodshed sieges caused, most ended with defenders being forced to surrender due to starvation. The Confederates at Vicksburg were reduced to eating mules and rats by the time they surrendered to Grant on July 4, 1863.

Siege of Petersburg

For 10 months between June 1864 and March 1865, Grant's troops besieged Lee's Confederate army at Petersburg, Virginia, ` a vital rail center. Grant built siege lines that extended for 35 miles (56 km). Heavily outnumbered, Lee's troops could not resist. At the Battle of Five Forks on April 1, 125,000 Union troops overwhelmed Lee's 10,000 men. Lee was forced to pull out of Petersburg and retreat. The defeat marked the beginning of the end of his army.

Union troops in the trenches during the Siege of Petersburg. Trench warfare was hard and dangerous.

May

May 10 Georgia
Confederate president Jefferson Davis is captured after a surprise raid on his camp at Irwinville.

May 13 Texas
In some of the last fighting of the war, Confederates defeat a small Union force at Palmito Ranch near Brownsville.

May 29 The new president, Andrew Johnson, grants an amnesty and pardon to Confederate soldiers, although murderers, arsonists, and others are excluded; former Rebels have to take an oath of allegiance to the U.S. Constitution.

Surrender of the Confederacy

General Lee's surrender to General Grant on April 9, 1865 was not the end of the Confederacy. It took several more weeks for the Civil War to come to an end.

↑ Confederate general Lee signs the document of surrender in the presence of Union general Grant.

TIMELINE **1865 JUNE–SEPTEMBER**

KEY: Politics | Land War | Sea War

June

June 2 Texas Having surrendered his army in Mississippi a few days earlier, Confederate general Edmund Kirby Smith flees to Mexico.

June 6 Washington, D.C. Confederate prisoners of war who are willing to swear allegiance to the Union are released.

June 23 Indian Territory The forces of General Stand Watie become the last Confederates to surrender.

July

July 7 Washington, D.C. Four people found guilty of conspiracy in Lincoln's assassination—Mary Surratt, Lewis Payne, David Herold, and George Atzerodt—are hanged at the Washington Penitentiary.

July 21 Massachusetts Harvard University holds a Commemoration Day to honor its war dead.

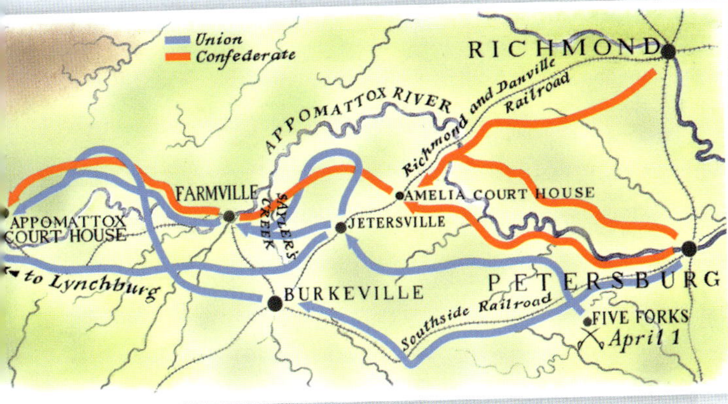

Exhausted Confederates struggled west in April 1865, but defeat loomed.

Although Ulysses S. Grant and Robert E. Lee commanded all the Union and Confederate armies, respectively, neither had the political authority to conclude a nationwide peace and end the war. The talks held at Appomattox Court House dealt only with the surrender of Lee's army in Virginia.

Politics of Surrender

President Abraham Lincoln made it clear to Grant that national peace was the sole responsibility of the president. There could be no talks about the surrender of the Confederacy as a nation because Lincoln and his administration had never accepted its claim to be a separate country nor recognized the legitimacy of Jefferson Davis's government.

KEY DATES

April 9, 1865 Talks between Lee and Grant to thrash out surrender terms.

April 26, 1865 Johnston signs new surrender document, acceptable to President Johnson.

May 1865 Most of remnants of the Confederacy finally surrender.

June 2, 1865 Confederate Jefferson Davis surrenders.

June 6, 1865 Confederate prisoners willing to swear allegiance to the U.S. are released.

June 10, 1865 President Johnson appoints new governors of Mississippi and Georgia.

June 23, 1865 Stand Watie is the last Confederate general to surrender.

August 20, 1866 President Andrew Johnson finally declares the Civil War is over.

August — **September**

September 12 Alabama
In the state capital, Montgomery, a convention agrees to restore relations with the federal government.

September 31 Alabama
The state convention abolishes slavery (about 10,000 Black Alabamians have fought for the Union army in the war).

The Ceremony of Surrender

On April 12, the Confederate Army of Northern Virginia laid down its arms and battle flags at a ceremony of formal surrender. As the Confederates came down the Union lines, bugles ordered the men in blue to "carry arms," a salute to their enemy, which the Southerners responded to in kind. It was a worthy end to the hard-fought war in Virginia.

Wilmer McLean's house in Appomattox Court House, where Lee surrendered to Grant on April 9, 1865.

Peace would come when each of the seceded states returned to the Union and accepted the Thirteenth Amendment of January 1865, which abolished slavery. That, however, depended on the surrender of the Confederate armies.

Confederate troops roll up their flag at the formal April 12 ceremony.

TIMELINE 1865 OCTOBER–DECEMBER

KEY: Politics | Land War | Sea War

October

November

November 10 Washington, D.C.
Confederate captain Henry Wirz is executed for war crimes committed while he was superintendent of the infamous Confederate prison of Andersonville, where thousands of Union troops died during the war.

Confederate Surrender

The surrender of the Army of Northern Virginia took three days from the first meeting between Lee and Grant in the parlor of Wilmer McLean's farmhouse in the village of Appomattox Court House on April 9. Lee agreed to Grant's terms.

Lee's surrender left three Confederate forces in the field: the army of General Joseph E. Johnston in North Carolina, that of General Richard Taylor in eastern Louisiana, Alabama, and Mississippi, and General Edmund Kirby Smith's army west of the Mississippi River. Johnston surrendered on April 26, Taylor in early May, and Kirby Smith later on May 26. The last Confederates surrendered in Indian Territory on June 23.

Final Capitulation

On June 6, Confederate prisoners of war willing to take the oath of allegiance were released. A few days later, President Andrew Johnson began to appoint governors for the former Confederate states. Despite the rapid move toward peace and reconciliation, it was not until August 20, 1866, that Johnson officially declared the Civil War was over, proclaiming that "The insurrection is at an end."

The Lost Cause

The Lost Cause myth developed among Southerners after the war. It included an idealized view of the Old South, where enslaved people and enslavers lived in harmony. It argued that the war was not caused by slavery but by Northern aggression. According to this view against impossible odds, the South had taken up an honorable fight for the states' rights.

Union general George Armstrong Custer accepts a flag of truce from a defeated Confederate officer in April 1865.

December

December 18 Washington, D.C.
The U.S. Congress ratifies the Thirteenth Amendment to the Constitution, which abolishes slavery as a legal institution in the United States.

Aftermath of the War

The attempt to reintegrate the former Confederacy into the Union was known as Reconstruction.

After the assassination of Abraham Lincoln in April 1865, Andrew Johnson became president. Johnson was sympathetic to the former slave states and wished to reintegrate them quickly. He was at odds with Republicans who dominated Congress, and he opposed the Fourteenth Amendment to the Constitution that offered freed enslaved people citizenship. He was impeached, charged with misconduct by the House of Representatives in 1868, but was cleared by one vote in the Senate.

1

Support for Freed Slaves

In 1868, Ulysses S. Grant was elected president. He supported the rights of former enslaved people and passed the Fifteenth Amendment, which forbade any state to deny citizens the vote "on account of race, color, or previous condition of servitude."

Grant also took on and reduced the power of the infamous Ku Klux Klan, which had emerged in 1865 to victimize and attack newly freed slaves. Under Grant, the states that had formed the Confederacy were all represented in Congress, some by former slaves.

Grant's successor in 1877 was President Rutherford B. Hayes. He disagreed with Grant's policies, and civil rights for African Americans in the Southern states were greatly diminished in the following decades.

2

KEY DATES

April, 1865 Soon after Confederate armies surrender, President Lincoln is assassinated. He is succeeded by Andrew Johnson, a Democrat from Tennessee.

Fall, 1865 Johnson proclaims that Reconstruction is over. He allows former Confederate officials to take seats in Congress.

1865-68 The Ku Klux Klan (KKK) unleashes a wave of violence directed against enslaved people of the former Confederacy.

1866 Elections bring a Radical Republican majority to Congress. The new Congress reverses Johnson's policies. It enforces the rights of formerly enslaved people, particularly the right to vote.

1869 Newly elected President Ulysses S. Grant uses the Enforcement Acts to root out the KKK.

1877 The final Federal forces are withdrawn from South Carolina, Louisiana, and Florida, ending the attempt to enforce Reconstruction on the former Confederacy.

1 Andrew Johnson was a former Democrat. As president, he was always going to find a Republican Congress difficult to deal with.

2 Republican congressman Thaddeus Stevens urges fellow members of the House to impeach President Andrew Johnson.

3 A contemporary print of Ku Klux Klan violence in North Carolina. President Grant moved decisively against the Klan.

4 An election poster for the 1876 election. After this election, troops were withdrawn from the former Confederate states and the political and civil rights of African Americans steadily worsened.

Glossary

abolition The ending of slavery; supporters of abolition were known as abolitionists.

artillery Heavy weapons such as cannon and mortars, which can fire large shells long distances.

blockade Measures aimed at preventing trade by using ships to intercept vessels heading toward port.

cavalry Soldiers who go into battle on horseback.

conscription Forcing ordinary civilians to join the army: both the Union and the Confederacy used conscription.

counterattack To respond to an attack by launching an attack of one's own.

emancipation Another word for "freedom."

garrison A group of soldiers who occupy a military post.

infantry Soldiers who fight on foot with small arms, as opposed to cavalry or artillery.

ironclad A Civil War ship that was protected by iron armor.

mine A hidden explosive device designed to destroy enemy transportation, such as ships.

mortar A type of cannon with a short-barrel designed to lob shells in an arc over defensive fortifications.

refugees People who have been displaced from their homes by war, starvation, or other disasters.

regiment A military unit that, when at full strength, includes 10 units of 100 men; in the Civil War, regiments were rarely at full strength.

secession Breaking away from the Union; states that seceded from the Union formed the Confederacy.

siege A campaign to capture a town or an army by surrounding it and cutting off its supplies.

skirmish A minor fight.

Further Resources

Books

Barber, James B. *Chicago to Appomattox: The 39th Illinois Infantry*. McFarland, 2022.

Cole, Taylor. *Researching the Causes of the American Civil War.* Rosen Publishing, 2019.

Howell, Sara. *The Civil War (Frontline Soldiers and Their Families)*. Gareth Stevens, 2016.

Keith, Phil and Tom Clavin. *To the Uttermost Ends of the Earth: The Greatest Sea Battle of the Civil War.* Hanover Square Press 2022.

Hardyman, Robyn. *What Caused the Civil War?* (*Why Wars Happened*). Gareth Stevens, 2017.

McGregor, Ian. *The US Civil War Battle by Battle.* Osprey, 2022.

Nussbaum, Ben. *Gettysburg: Three Days that Saved the United States*. Fox Chapel Publishing, 2022.

Randolph, Joanne. *Mr. Lincoln.* Rosen Publishing, 2019.

Randolph, Joanne. *The Civil War and Reconstruction.* Rosen Publishing, 2019.

Smithsonian Museum. *The Civil War: A Visual History.* Dorling Kindersley, 2015.

Steele, Philip. *Did Any Good Come Out of The Civil War?* Rosen Publishing, 2016.

Websites

kids.nationalgeographic.com/history/article/gettysburg
A good introduction from National Geographic to this key battle.

kids.britannica.com/kids/article/American-Civil-War/352967
Check out more facts from Britannica Kids about the Civil War.

www.history.com/topics/american-civil-war
General articles on the Civil War.

www.pbs.org/civilwar
PBS site supporting the Ken Burns film *The Civil War.*

www.civilwar.si.edu
The Smithsonian Institution's Civil War collections, with essays, images, and other primary sources.

Index